# Warbirds

## fotofax

# JAGUAR

Michael J. Gething

**Front cover illustration:**
Resplendent in the desert
camouflage applied for service
in Chad, this Armée de l'Air
Jaguar-A of EC2/11 'Vosges' is
seen carrying the French
version of the external fuel tank,
with stub fins and endplates.
(Sergeant G. Rolie/SIRPA-Air)

**Back cover illustrations:**
**Top:** This quartet of Jaguar
GR.1As from 6 Sqn RAF, shows
a wide variety of the weaponry
now used by the RAF's
contracted Jaguar force,
including Sidewinder AAMs,
Paveway laser-guided bombs,
264 gallon drop tanks, Phimat
chaff dispensers and 1,000lb
bombs. (Geoff Lee, BAe
Kingston)
**Below:** A Jaguar International
OS model from the Sultan of
Oman's Air Force roars low over
the desert on exercise. (BAe
Warton)

# JAGUAR

## Michael J. Gething

ARMS AND
ARMOUR

# INTRODUCTION

First published in Great Britain in 1989 by Arms and Armour Press, Artillery House, Artillery Row, London SW1P 1RT.

Distributed in the USA by Sterling Publishing Co. Inc., 2 Park Avenue, New York, NY 10016.

Distributed in Australia by Capricorn Link (Australia) Pty. Ltd., P.O. Box 665, Lane Cove, New South Wales 2066, Australia.

British Library Cataloguing in Publication Data:
Gething, Michael J.
Jaguar
1. SEPECAT Jaguar aeroplanes
I. Title.    II. Series
623.74'63
ISBN 0-85368-951-2

Line drawings by James Goulding.

Designed and edited by DAG Publications Ltd. Designed by David Gibbons; edited by Michael Boxall; layout by Cilla Eurich; typeset by Ronset Typesetters Ltd, Darwen, Lancashire, and by Typesetters (Birmingham) Limited, Warley, West Midlands; camerawork by M&E Reproductions, North Fambridge, Essex; printed and bound in Great Britain by The Alden Press Limited, Oxford.

**2.** Fast but not too low, this pair of Jaguar GR.1s from 6 Sqn RAF, come in for a simulated attack in murky weather. (Image in Industry/BAe Warton)

The Jaguar is a product of the mid-1960s and is claimed to be the first international collaborative project to be set up for a military combat aircraft. France had a requirement for a combat trainer and light attack aircraft (Ecole de Combat d'Appui Tactique – ECAT), while in the United Kingdom the RAF was looking to replace the Gnat T.1 and the Hunter F.6/T.7 combination through its Air Staff Target (later Requirement) 362.

With the 'Entente CONcordial' recently signed, the French and UK Ministers of Defence of the day, Pierre Messmer and Peter Thorneycroft, thought it would make sense to merge their requirements. The respective air staffs were so instructed. At this time (late 1964) Breguet Aviation's Br.121 design had been selected for ECAT and as the RAF were able to compress their requirements around this aircraft, it was selected as the basis for what became Jaguar. Obviously a compromise, the British Aircraft Corporation – BAC – were offered design leadership on the Anglo-French Variable Geometry (AFVG) aircraft to be based on their P45 design. Sadly, the French withdrew in 1967 and it was later in the decade that the MRCA (Tornado) finally saw light of day (see Warbirds Illustrated No.42).

The Memorandum of Understanding covering both Jaguar and AFVG was signed in May 1965 and after several changes and amendments to numbers the total number of aircraft required was defined as 40 Ecole (E) and 160 Appui (A) versions (originally 75 of each type were required) for L'Armée de l'Air, 35 B trainer models (originally 110) and 165 S (strike) models (originally 90) for the RAF – a total of 400 aircraft. Initially there was provision for 40 Maritime (M) and ten E versions for L'Aéronavale, but when they later pulled out of the project, the 40 Jaguar-M aircraft in the programme were rescheduled as A models for the L'Armée de l'Air. The switch of RAF emphasis from the trainer to the strike role led to the development of a new trainer, the HS.1182, more widely known now as the Hawk.

A joint company, the Société Européenne de Production de l'Avion Ecole Combat et d'Appui Tactique – SEPECAT, was set up to produce the aircraft. The worksplit was 50:50 with no duplication of manufacture, although a final assembly line was established in each country. The power plant, based on a Rolls-Royce design, the RB172, (already selected for ECAT) was also jointly produced, by Rolls-Royce and Turboméca of France.

In France, Avions Marcel Dassault were livid that Breguet had beaten them to the ECAT contract but when, in 1967, they absorbed Breguet Aviation they found Jaguar almost an embarrassment, competing as it did with versions of the Mirage family. Indeed, Jaguar and the Mirage F1 competed against each other in several export competitions, including India (where Jaguar won). It must be said that, although initially, export drives were a SEPECAT venture, the four export sales recorded for Jaguar (Ecuador, Oman, India and Nigeria) have all been British Aerospace led. That said, Dassault, when competing Mirage with Jaguar, could not lose: they either secured the whole contract or half of the contract, if Jaguar won!

Interestingly enough, the export model – known as Jaguar International – was based on the RAF's S model which was always a more sophisticated weapons system than the French A model equivalent. Production is now virtually complete, except in

India (where a further 31 may yet be built by Hindustan Aeronautics Ltd). Any further export sales will be made with ex-RAF or L'Armée de l'Air aircraft, refurbished as required.

In service, Jaguar has been popular with its pilots and a more sophisticated aircraft than the F-100 Super Sabre, Mystère IV-A, Hunter FGA.9 and Canberra B(I).8 it replaced. The RAF have, over the years, improved the Jaguar's navigation/attack system and added other weapons/avionics refinements (adding the suffix A to the designated variant number), as have the French. Although now starting to be replaced both in France (by the Mirage 2000N) and in the UK (by the Tornado GR.1), both countries are expected to retain Jaguars in service into the 21st century in limited numbers.

**3.** Brand-new and shiny, the first Jaguar prototype, a French trainer, EO1, sits on the ground at Istres in 1968. Although a two-seater, the sleek shape of the aircraft is evident and, if the old adage, 'if it looks good, it is good' needed confirmation, Jaguar would provide it. (BAe Warton)

**4.** First prototype Jaguar EO1 in the air on its maiden flight on 8 September 1968, with Breguet

▲3   ▼4

chief test pilot, Bernard Witt, at the controls. The clean configuration emphasizes the thoroughbred look of the aircraft. Witt's comment after the flight was simple and direct. 'Jaguar flies very well. I had no problems.' (BAe Warton)

I have been close to the Jaguar since 1971 and so have been able to draw upon my photographic archives collected over the years. To that end, I must acknowledge the help and assistance given by the various RAF squadrons (and specifically the Press Liaison Team from RAF Lossiemouth), the UK MoD, the French MoD public relations organization (SIRPA-Air) and my French colleague, Alexandra Schwartzbrod. On the industry side, special thanks must go to Geoffrey Hill (now retired) and David Kamiya from BAe's Military Aircraft Division at Warton, and, from across the Channel, Christine Mougin at Avions Marcel Dassault-Breguet Aviation and Colonel Jean-Claude Salvinien of Aérospatiale's Missiles' Division. Among other individuals whose photographic work is included here, I must thank Barry Ellson of RAF Germany, Malcolm English, Tim Wrixon and Geoff Lee of British Aerospace Kingston.

**5 ▲**

**5.** After a flight time of 25 minutes, Jaguar EO1 lands at Istres to complete its maiden flight. The French national markings remained virtually unchanged during its career, with the exception that the rudder flash of blue, white and red was deleted and the size of the roundels was reduced slightly. (BAe Warton)

**6.** The second French trainer prototype, Jaguar EO2, coded 'C' just aft of the auxiliary inlet doors on the engine intake, on an early test flight. The clean lines of the aircraft, unencumbered by stores pylons and weapons or tanks shows its origin as an advanced jet trainer. (AMD-BA)

**6 ▼**

▲7   ▼8

▼9

**7.** Wearing the white 'buzz number' of its Paris air show identification, Bernard Witt deploys the drag 'chute on landing after a display at Le Bourget in 1969. The white surrounds to the ejection seat markings have disappeared, as has the rudder flash. (BAe Warton)

**8.** The first French single-seat prototype, Jaguar AO3, coded 'D', takes to the air on its maiden flight on 29 March 1969 in standard Armée de l'Air camouflage of the time. (AMD-BA)

**9.** Seen in a rare formation shot, single-seat prototype AO3 formates with EO1 and EO2 in 1969. The clean lines of both versions are emphasized in this view. Jaguar EO1 was later to loose the fin flash on its rudder. (AMD-BA)

**10.** Jaguar AO4 waits on the ground prior to taxiing out for a test flight in 1969. The dark fin tip houses the UHF/VHF radio antennae. This aircraft, supported by a French ground crew and flown by Jimmy Dell, appeared as part of the 57th anniversary celebrations of the RAF Central Flying School at Little Rissington in 1969 (BAe Warton)

**11.** The main role of AO4 during the test programme was the clearance of weapons and stores carriage and weapon-firing. Here it is seen with twin stores carriers, each with a pair of 1,000lb free-fall GP bombs on the inboard pylons. Note the extended trailing edge of the stores pylon. (Breguet)

**12.** In 1965, the French Navy had intended that the Jaguar replace its Etendard IVs in service with L'Aéronavale. Here the sole naval Jaguar prototype, MO5, is seen on the forward deck lift of the carrier *Clemenceau*. (BAe Warton)

10▲  11▼

12▼

▲13  ▼14

**13.** Jaguar MO5 sits on *Clemenceau*'s forward catapult, ready to launch during carrier trials off Lorient in October 1971. Prior to participating in these trials, MO5 had done dummy take-offs and landings from RAE Bedford in the UK. (BAe Warton)

**14.** Seconds after the last picture was taken, MO5, afterburners alight, roars off *Clemenceau*'s flight deck. Note that the main undercarriage has single wheels, while the nose gear is a twin-wheel installation; the configuration is vice versa on all other versions. (BAe Warton)

**15.** This view of MO5 taking the wire emphasizes the Jaguar-M's alternate undercarriage configuration. The carrier trials proved the type's suitability for operations at sea, but in 1973 this version was cancelled in favour of the Super Etendard. (Breguet)

**16.** The first British single-seater to fly (and fifth in the series) was Jaguar SO6, which made its maiden flight on 12 October 1969, with the chief test pilot of BAC's Preston Division, Jimmy Dell, at the controls. At this time, it differed externally very little from the French A model, with its pointed nose and no RWR fairing on the fin. Note the extended air brakes, slotted to increase turbulence and, thus, drag. (BAe Warton)

**17.** Jaguar SO6, seen in company with second S model, SO7 (which flew for the first time on 12 June 1970) early in the flight test programme. Jaguar SO7 was the first aircraft to be fitted with the Elliott (now GEC Avionics) NAVWASS. (BAe Warton)

15▲   16▼

17▼

▲18

**18.** Later in the development of the Jaguar, SO7 was fitted with the fin-mounted RWR and the aerodynamic shape of the LRMTS 'window' in the nose. Here it has released a 1,000lb free-fall GP bomb on a straight- and-level pass at an airspeed of 450 knots. The centreline pylon carries a 264 gallon external fuel tank. (BAe Warton)

**19.** With the rear cockpit fitted with data-recording equipment, Paul Millett takes the first British two-seat Jaguar, BO8 (RAF designation T.2) for its maiden flight on 30 August 1971. The flight lasted 49 minutes and BO8 was supersonic for part of that time.

Being the last of the prototypes, much of the aircraft was constructed of production parts. (BAe Warton)

▼19

20▲   21▼

**20.** Now re-painted with B-type roundels, BO8 is seen here deploying its drag 'chute for landing on rough grass at A&AEE Boscombe Down during rough field trials. It is carrying a pair of 264 gallon drop tanks on the inboard pylons and camera/date-link equipment pods on the outer pylons. (BAe Warton)

**21.** Here the first production Jaguar GR.1 (S1 – XX108) is seen during engine-running tests at Warton in September 1972. It is still in primer finish, with the camouflage and RAF insignia yet to be applied. Note the mesh cover to the air intakes to reduce the risk of FOD (foreign object digestion) during the runs. At this stage neither the LRMTS or RWR has been fitted. (BAe Warton)

**22.** Now painted, the first production Jaguar GR.1 is shown landing after its maiden flight from Warton on 11 October 1972 with BAC Military Aircraft Division's deputy chief test pilot, Tim Ferguson, at the controls. The flight lasted 1 hour 11 minutes, being supersonic for part of the time. (BAe Warton)

22▼

**▲23 ▼24**

**23.** The Jaguar's 'office'. In this case an RAF GR.1 fitted with the Ferranti FIN1064 inertial navigation system. The system control and display unit is positioned on the port coaming (upper left) where the pilot can see and operate it without having to go 'head down' for long periods. Central in the picture is the moving map display, above which can be seen the projector for the head-up display. Basic flight instruments are to the left of the moving map display, engine instruments to the right. (Ferranti International)

**24.** Jaguar BO8 seen in one of Warton's hangars with an array of representative weapons displayed. From front to back, left to right, are (first row) 68mm unguided air-to-ground rockets; (second row) four 4lb practice bombs, eight 28lb practice bombs and a further four 4lb practice bombs; (third row) CBLS, AIM-9B Sidewinder AAM, Lepus flare, 30mm ADEN cannon with ammunition and the same in reverse; (fourth row) 264 Imp gall fuel tank, four Matra 155 rocket pods and the same in reverse; (fifth row) four 1,000lb GP bombs each side; and behind the outer pylons two 1,000lb retarded GP bombs. The aircraft carries two 264 Imp gall fuel tanks. (BAe Warton)

**25.** Although component manufacture of Jaguar was split 50:50 without duplication, there were two assembly lines. BAC built the wings, tail unit, rear-fuselage and engine intakes. This photograph depicts the British line at Warton, showing the final assembly with twelve aircraft almost complete. (BAe Warton)

**26.** The French share of production was the nose and centre fuselage, plus the undercarriage. This photograph shows the French final assembly line at Colombiers on Toulouse-Blagnac airport in south-west France.(Breguet)

▲27 ▼28

**27.** Seen outside its hardened aircraft shelter at Nancy, this Jaguar-A of EC3/3 'Ardennes' shows the Aérospatiale AS.37 Martel anti-radiation missile, used in the 'Wild Weasel' role of defence-suppression, mounted under the fuselage. The inner pylons carry 1,200-litre fuel tanks while the outboard pylons have an ECM pod. (J. P. Gauthier/ SIRPA-Air)

**28.** One of the first A models to enter service with EC1/7 'Provence', this Jaguar-A is seen 'clean' on the apron at RAF Lossiemouth in 1973. The Wing (Escadre) badge is seen on the starboard side of the fin. (Tim Wrixon)

▼29

**29.** This 1979 photograph shows clearly the differences between the French-A (from EC1/7 with the Escadron badge on the port side of the fin) and the RAF's S model, designated Jaguar GR.1. The French aircraft retains a clean nose and fin, while the RAF Jaguar has the 'chisel' nose housing the LRMTS and a fin-mounted fairing for the RWR. Note also, the differing styles of strake at the rear of the 1,200-litre fuel tanks carried by both aircraft. (RAF Germany)

30▲

**30.** This trio of Jaguar-B trainers from EC1/7 'Provence' show the clean lines of the Jaguar to perfection. The aircraft closest to the camera is an early example (the 13th) of this variant. The unit is due to re-equip with the Mirage 2000N shortly. (AMD-BA)

**31.** This pair of Jaguar As are from the EC2/7 'Argonne', the squadron which now acts as the operational conversion unit for the Jaguar in French service.

Although the aircraft here carry no underwing stores, the centreline and outer-wing pylons are visible. (SIRPA-Air)

**32.** This Jaguar-E trainer from EC2/7 displays the 'Archer in a Ring' badge of the 'Argonne' Escadron. The stalky undercarriage with low-pressure tyres, which allows it to use rough airstrips, is clearly visible. (SIRPA-Air)

◀31

32▼

▲33
33. A view of a Jaguar-E of EC2/7 shows the other side of the aircraft, seen in a dispersal revetment at RAF Bruggen during an exchange visit in 1979. Note the 1,200-litre fuel tanks, and the open panel of the gunbay housing a 30mm DEFA 553 cannon. (RAF Germany)

34. A Jaguar-A from EC3/7 'Languedoc' is shown here carrying eighteen Thomson Brandt BAP 100 runway denial weapons under the fuselage, external fuel tanks on the inner pylons and an ECM pod on the outer pylon. (SIRPA-Air)

▼34

**35.** Another view of an EC3/7 single-seater shows the external fuel tanks and ECM pods under the wing. This unit is assigned to the nuclear strike role, armed with the AN52 free-fall nuclear weapon and is due to be replaced by the Mirage 2000N imminently. (J. P. Gauthier/SIRPA-Air)

**36.** Seen participating in the RAF's Tactical Fighter Meet in 1986, this Jaguar-A of EC4/7 'Limousin' carries external fuel tanks on the inner pylons, Matra Phimat chaff/flare dispensers on the outer pylons and a practice bomb-carrier on the centreline. (Malcolm English)

**37.** With a Phamtom, Tornado GR.1 and an RAF Jaguar GR.1 in the background, this Jaguar-A of EC4/7 waits to take-off during the RAF's Tactical Fighter Meet at RAF Waddington in 1986. This unit is more usually dedicated to nuclear strike duties from its base at Istres-le-Tubé and is part of the French Force d'Intervention Aérienne. (RAF Waddington)

▲38  ▼39

▼40

**38.** A Jaguar-A of EC1/11 'Roussillon' takes-off from its base at Toul-Rosières on a training flight. The large store under the fuselage appears to be either an in-flight refuelling 'buddy pack' or a target drogue of some description. (SIRPA-Air)

**39.** Seen on the apron at Toul, this Jaguar-A of EC1/11 carries its external fuel tank on the centreline stores pylons and a 250kg bomb can be seen on a multiple stores rack on the inner pylon. The Escadron is tasked with conventional strike duties. (SIRPA-Air)

**40.** With the wing of their C-135F tanker in the foreground, a Jaguar-A and an E model of EC2/11 'Vosges', in desert camouflage, are deploying to Chad in Africa during the French support operations in 1986. (G. Rolle/SIRPA-Air)

**41.** This line-up of aircraft in Chad in 1986 shows three Jaguar As and a single Jaguar-E, all from EC2/11 and in desert camouflage, in company with a pair of Mirage F1-C-200 fighters. Jaguars of this unit took part in the raid on the Libyan-held airfield at Ouadi Doum on 16 February 1986, using BAP 100 runway-cratering bombs. (G. Rolle/SIRPA-Air)

**42.** A Jaguar-A of EC3/11 'Corse' in desert camouflage with BAT 120 area-denial weapons on the centreline. Based at Toul, the Escadron is tasked with a conventional strike role. Note the bulge under the nose, immediately aft of the pitot tube, which contains a laser rangefinder. (SIRPA-Air)

**43.** With a single-seater for company, a Jaguar-E of EC3/11 takes on fuel from a Boeing C-135F tanker. This aircraft carries outer wing chaff/flare dispensers and centreline fuel tanks. The Jaguar-A in the foreground carries the centreline fuel tank and a rocket pod on the outer wing pylon. Note the rear strake to the pylon not found on the RAF's Jaguars. (SIRPA-Air)

41▲   42▼

40▼

# JAGUAR GR.1A

of 6 Sqn RAF Cottesmore, 1988. The 'wraparound' camouflage is of dark-green and dark sea-grey. Apart from the avionics modifications and addition of chaff dispensers, this version has now been cleared to carry the Phimat chaff/flare dispenser and ALQ-101-10 ECM pod, AIM-9 Sidewinder missiles and Paveway II laser-guided bombs. For clarity, none of these stores is shown here.

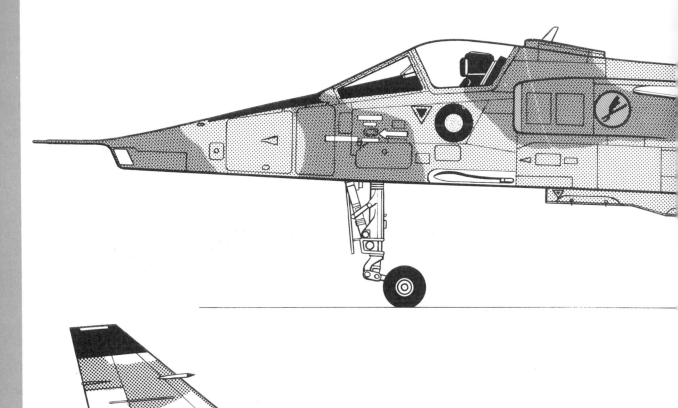

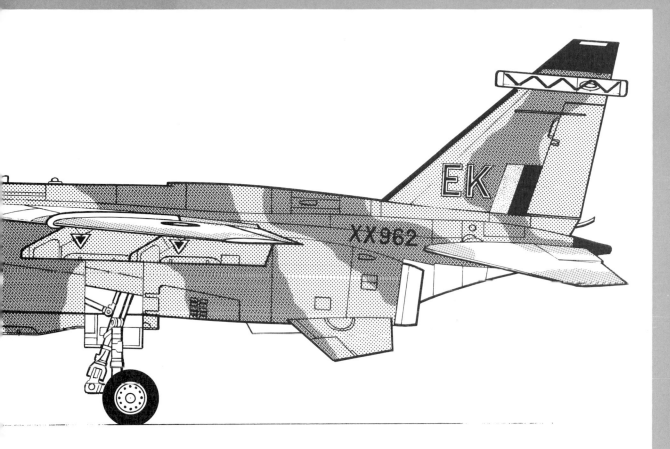

## JAGUAR-A

of EC-4/11 'Jura', L'Armée de l'Air, Bordeaux-Mérignac, 1988. The aircraft is depicted in the desert camouflage used for aircraft deployed into Chad, the underside in this case being a semi-gloss silver.

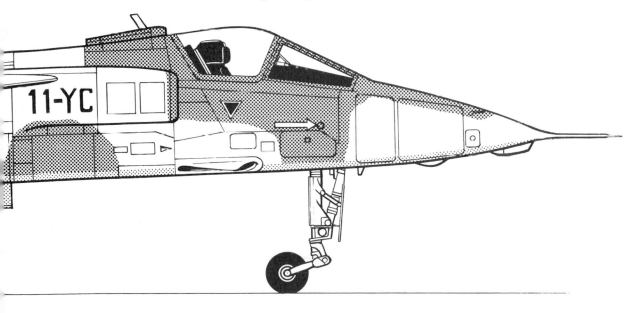

# SPECIFICATIONS

| | Jaguar-A | Jaguar-S (GR.1) | Jaguar-M | Jaguar-E | Jaguar-B (T.2) |
|---|---|---|---|---|---|
| Wingspan | 28ft 6in | 28ft 6in | 28ft 6in | 28ft 6in | 28ft 6in |
| Length (incl. probe) | 55ft 2.5in | 55ft 2.5in | 55ft 2.5in | 57ft 6.25in | 57ft 6.25in |
| Height | 16ft 0.5in | 16ft 0.5in | 16ft 0.5in | 16ft 0.5in | 16ft 0.5in |
| Weight (empty) | 15,432lb | 15,432lb | 15,432lb | 15,432lb | 15,432lb |
| Weight (max. take-off) | 24,149lb | 24,149lb | 24,149lb | 24,149lb | 24,149lb |
| Armament | 2×30mm DEFA 553 cannon | 2×30mm ADEN cannon | 2×30mm DEFA 553 cannon | 2×30mm DEFA cannon | 1×30mm ADEN cannon |
| | plus up to 2,500lb of stores on centreline and each inboard pylon, and up to 1,250lb of stores on each external pylon; with a maximum external payload of 10,500lb | | | | |
| Power plants: | All have Rolls-Royce/Turboméca Adour turbofans | | | | |
| current models | Mk 102 | Mk 104 | Mk 102 | Mk 102 | Mk 104 |
| rated at (dry) | 5,115lb | 5,260lb | 5,115lb | 5,115lb | 5,260lb |
| and (reheat) | 7,305lb | 8,600lb | 7,305lb | 7,305lb | 8,600lb |

Export power plants: the Adour Mk 804 equates to Mk 104, but uprated to 5,320lb st (dry) and 8,040lb with afterburning; while the Mk 811 is rated at 5,520lb st (dry) and 9,270lb st with afterburning. The Mk 815C is a Mk 804 uprated to Mk 811 performance by conversion at overhaul.

Max. level speed:
at sea level Mach 1.1 (729kts, 840mph) for all variants
at 36,000ft Mach 1.6 (917kts, 1,056mph) for all variants.

Typical attack radii (applicable to Jaguar-A, -S (GR.1) and International -S models):

| | |
|---|---|
| (hi-lo-hi, internal fuel) | 460nm (530 miles) |
| (hi-lo-hi, with external fuel) | 760nm (875 miles) |
| (lo-lo-lo, internal fuel) | 290nm (334 miles) |
| (lo-lo-lo, with external fuel) | 495nm (570 miles) |

Ferry range with external fuel: 1,902nm (2,190 miles)

# VARIANTS

**Jaguar-A** (Fr: Appui – attack)
Single-seat attack fighter. Martin-Baker Mk 4 ejection seat. Avionics – ESD RDN 72 Doppler radar, Thomson-CSF laser rangefinder (with an Alcatel CILAS ITAY 139 laser illuminator); SFIM 153-6 twin-gyro inertial platform; Crouzet Type 90 navigation computer; Thomson-CSF Type 31 weapons-aiming computer; Dassault fire-control computer; Thomson-CSF BF radar warning receiver (RWR); Alkan/Lacroix LC530 40mm chaff/flare dispensers.
Prototypes A03 and A04:    2
Production A1 to A160:   160=162 built.

**Jaguar-E** (Fr: Ecole – trainer)
Two-seat operational trainer. 2 × Martin-Baker Mk 4 ejection seats. Avionics – as Jaguar-A.
Prototypes E01 and E02:    2
Production E1 to E40:    40=42 built.

**Jaguar-S** (UK)
Single-seat attack fighter. RAF designation **GR.1/GR.1A.** Martin-Baker Mk 9 ejection seat.
*Avionics GR.1*: Marconi (now GEC) Avionics digital/inertial Navigation And Weapons-Aiming SubSystem (NAVWASS) based on an MCS 920M digital computer; Marconi (now GEC) Avionics air-data computer; Ferranti Type 105 laser ranger and Type 106 marked-target seeker (known by the joint acronym of LRMTS); Smiths Industries Head-Up Display (HUD) with a three-gyro inertial platform; and the Marconi Defence Systems ARI.18223 radar warning receiver in a tail-fin fairing.

*Avionics GR.1A* – For the mid-life update, elements of NAVWASS were replaced by the Ferranti FIN 1064 digital nav/attack system from 1981 onwards, thus reducing weight (by 50kg) and size and increasing its memory capacity from 16K to 64K. This also includes provision for AIM-9 Sidewinder AAMs, Phimat chaff/flare dispenser, Westinghouse ALQ-101 jamming pod and two Tracor chaff/flare dispensers on 'scab' mounts under the rear fuselage.

| | | |
|---|---|---|
| Prototypes: | XW560 and XW563 | 2 |
| Production: | XX108-XX122 | 15 |
| | XX719-XX768 | 50 |
| | XX817-XX827 | 11 |
| | XX955-XX979 | 25 |
| | XZ101-XZ120 | 20 |
| | XZ355-XZ378 | 24 |
| | XZ381-XZ400 | 20 |
| | | =167 built. |

**Jaguar-B** (UK)
Two-seat operational conversion trainer. RAF designation **T.2/T.2A.** 2 × Martin-Baker Mk 9 ejection seats. Avionics T.2 – as for Jaguar GR.1, but without the RWR and LRMTS. The GR.1A mid-life update also applies to the T.2A.

| | | |
|---|---|---|
| Prototype: | XW566 | 1 |
| Production: | XX136-XX150 | 15 |
| | XX828-XX847 | 20 |
| | XX915-XX916 (for ETPS) | 2 |
| | ZB615 (attrition for ETPS) | 1 |
| | | =39 built. |

**Jaguar-M** (Fr: Maritime – naval)
Single-seat naval strike fighter. Martin-Baker Mk 4 ejection seat. Avionics – as for Jaguar-A. Project abandoned 1973 in favour of Dassault-Breguet Super Etendard.
Prototype M05:  1 built.

**Jaguar International**
Single-seat attack fighter, basically the Jaguar-S (GR.1) in all respects except where indicated. Trainers equivalent to Jaguar-B (T.2). In service with:

*Ecuador* (with Adour Mk 804)
| | |
|---|---|
| Single-seat: | 10 |
| Trainers: | 2 |
| | =12 built. |

*India:* Known as Shamsher (Hindi for 'brave warrior') in IAF service. Avionics – Smiths Industries Type 1301 HUD and digital weapons-aiming computer (as fitted in Sea Harrier FRS.1); SAGEM ULISS-82 inertial navigation system (from Batch 2, aircraft 10); Ferranti COMED 2045 combined map and electronic display; and a MIL STD 1553 dual-redundant digital data bus. Some eight aircraft (with more to come if the fourth batch is ordered) are fitted with Thomson-CSF Agave radar in modified nose with Ferranti Type 105 laser ranger in a chin-mounted fairing.

Batch 1: UK-built (with Adour Mk 804)

| | |
|---|---|
| Single-seat IS: | 35 |
| Trainer IB: | 5 |

Batch 2: HAL transition batch (with Adour Mk 811)

| | |
|---|---|
| Single-seat IS: | 29 |
| IM: | 6 |
| Trainer IB: | 10 |

Batch 3: HAL-built (with Adour Mk 811)

| | |
|---|---|
| Single-seat IS: | 29 |
| IM: | 2 |

Batch 4: HAL-built (with Adour Mk 811)

| | |
|---|---|
| | 31 |
| | =147 built. |

(As at early 1989, Indian sources suggest this fourth batch is agreed, but no formal contract exists.)

The following sixteen GR.1 and two T.2 RAF aircraft (with Mk 102 engines) on loan to IAF to allow Jaguar to enter service swiftly. Since returned between June 1982 and April 1984. (Compiled from a correlation of manufacturer's BARG and Air-Britain records.) JI001 (XX138-T.2), JI002 (XX143-T.2), JI003 (XX117), JI004 (XX720), JI005 (XX115), JI006 (XZ397)*, JI007 (XZ398), JI008 (XX116), JI009 (XX728), JI010 (XX725), JI011 (XX111)**, JI012 (XX729), JI013 (XX736), JI014 (XX734), JI015 (XX737), JI016 (XX738), JI017 (XX740)***, JI018 (XX118).

*Lost in India 16 April 1981. **Lost in India 10 May 1982. ***Sold to Oman as an attrition replacement in November 1986.

Nigeria (with Adour Mk 811)

| | |
|---|---|
| Single-seat: | 13 |
| Trainers: | 5 |
| | =18 built. |

Oman

Batch 1 (with Adour Mk 804)*

| | |
|---|---|
| Single-seat: | 10 |
| Trainers: | 2 |

Batch 2 (with Adour Mk 811)

| | |
|---|---|
| Single-seat: | 10 |
| Trainers: | 2 |
| | =24 built. |

*Subsequently upgraded to Mk 815 standard. Second batch had provision for overwing hardpoints, while second batch trainers had AAR probe in place of nose pitot tube.

GRAND PRODUCTION TOTAL=612 built.

## WEAPONS CLEARED FOR CARRIAGE

**Internal Armament**
Jaguar—A/EM: 2×30mm DEFA 553 cannon with 150rpg.
Jaguar—S/IntS: 2×30mm ADEN cannon with 150rpg.
Jaguar—B/IntB: 1×30mm ADEN cannon with 150rpg.

**External Armament**
Carried on five external stores hardpoints: fuselage centreline and inboard underwing pylons stressed to carry 2,500lb, with provision for carriage of 264 Imp. gallon fuel tanks; outboard underwing pylons stressed to carry 1,250lb. Overwing pylons (above inboard underwing pylons) for the carriage of air-to-air missiles, such as Sidewinder or Magic.

Among the stores cleared for carriage by the Jaguar are:
**Air-to-air missiles:** AIM-9B/P Sidewinder, Matra R.550 Magic 1/2.
**Air-to-surface missiles:** AGM-84 Harpoon anti-ship missile (ASM); AS.67 Martel anti-radar missile (ARM); AJ168 TV Martel; AS.30/30L (latter in conjunction with ATLIS II laser designator pod); AM.39 Exocet ASM; Kormoran ASM; Sea Eagle ASM; Alarm ARM; Mk 13/18 Paveway II laser-guided bomb (LGB) and Matra BGL 250, 400 and 1000 Arole laser-guided bombs.
**Bombs:** Matra Durandal anti runway bomb; Thomson Brandt BAP-100 cratering system and BAT-120 area denial system; Hunting CMD18 [formerly known as the JP233 dispenser (short)] runway denial system; Hunting BL755 cluster bomb; Matra Belouga cluster bomb; British 1,000lb GP bomb; Matra/SAMP retarded bomb (1,000 & 500lb versions); Matra BEU 2 551lb bomb and 4, 20, 28lb and SB practice bombs (sometimes in a CBLS [Carrier, Bombs, Light Stores] pod).
**Nuclear Weapons:** AN.52 free-fall nuclear bomb (France) and WE-177 free-fall nuclear bomb (UK).
**Rocket pods:** Matra 155 launcher (18×68mm rockets); Matra RL F2 launcher (6×68mm rockets); Thomson Brandt LR 100–6 (6×100mm rockets) and Thomson Brandt LR 100–4 (4× 100mm rockets).
**Other stores:** Matra Phimat chaff/flare dispenser; Lepus flares; various laser designator pods; Westinghouse ALQ—101-10 ECM pod, other ECM and reconnaissance pods.

(Note: this list is not fully comprehensive.)

## SQUADRON ALLOCATIONS AND BASES: FRANCE

Each Wing (Escadre de Chasse – EC) is divided into Squadrons (Escadrons) which, as well as its number, has assigned a name, usually a region of France; thus the first squadron of the 3rd Wing would be written EC1/3. The aircraft carry wing/squadron identity codes consisting of the Wing number and Squadron code letter plus the individual aircraft code letter, e.g., 3-KL. In the following table, only the Wing/Squadron combination is shown.

| Unit | Code | Base | Role |
|---|---|---|---|
| 3e Escadre de Chasse | | | |
| EC1/3 Ardennes | 3-K | Nancy-Ochey | Defence suppression |
| 7e Escadre de Chasse | | | |
| EC1/7 Provence | 7-H | St-Dizier-Robinson | Nuclear strike |
| EC2/7 Argonne | 7-P | „ | OCU |
| EC3/7 Languedoc | 7-I | „ | Nuclear strike |
| EC4/7 Limousin | 7-N | Istres-le-Tubé | Nuclear strike*/** |
| 11e Escadre de Chasse | | | |
| EC1/11 Roussillon | 11-E | Toul-Rosières | Conventional strike |
| EC2/11 Vosges | 11-M | „ | ECM |
| EC3/11 Corse | 11-R | „ | Conventional strike |
| EC4/11 Jura | 11-Y | Bordeaux-Mérignac | Conventional strike** |

*This will be the first Jaguar-A unit to convert to the Mirage 2000N during the course of 1990.
**These two units comprise the airborne strike element of the French Force d'Intervention Aérienne.

## SQUADRON ALLOCATIONS AND BASES: UNITED KINGDOM

Current RAF Jaguar units carry a two-letter code on the fin, the first letter being the Squadron identification and the second letter the individual coding. Two-figure tail numbers rather than letters are used by 226 OCU. Currently in service are the following.

| Unit | Code | Base | Role |
|---|---|---|---|
| 6 Sqn RAF* | E | Coltishall, UK | Conventional strike |
| 41 Sqn RAF* | F** | | Tactical Recce*** |
| 54 Sqn RAF* | G | | Conventional strike |
| 226 OCU RAF | — | Lossiemouth, UK | OCU |

*Assigned to Allied Command Europe (ACE) Mobile Force.
**Although allocated, not apparently used.
***Will re-equip with reconnaissance Tornados in 1989.

Former Jaguar Squadrons (now equipped with Tornado GR.1):

| Unit | Code | Base | Role |
|---|---|---|---|
| 2 Sqn RAF (1976–88) | ? | Laarbruch, FRG | Tactical Recce* |
| 14 Sqn RAF (1975–85) | A | Bruggen, FRG | Conv/nuclear strike |
| 17 Sqn RAF (1975–85) | B | | |
| 20 Sqn RAF (1977–84) | C | | |
| 31 Sqn RAF (1975–84) | D | | |

*Re-equipped with Tornado GR.1 modified for the reconnaissance mission in early 1989.

## OVERSEAS OPERATORS

| Country | Unit | Base | Role |
|---|---|---|---|
| ECUADOR | Escuadron de Combate 2111 Aguilas (Eagles) | Base Aerea Militar Tauro near Quito | Attack/training |
| INDIA | 5 Sqn IAF | Ambalah | Conventional strike |
| | 6 Sqn IAF* | Poona | Maritime strike |
| | 14 Sqn IAF | Ambalah | Conventional strike |
| | 16 Sqn IAF | Gorakhpur | Conventional strike |
| | 27 Sqn IAF | Gorakhpur | Conventional strike |
| NIGERIA | ? Sqn NAF | Mukurdi | Strike/ reconnaissance |
| OMAN | 8 Sqn SOAF | Masirah AB | Attack/training |
| | 20 Sqn SOAF | Masirah AB | Attack/training |

*Composite unit: A Flight with Agave-Jaguar (Shamsher); B Flight with Canberra B(I).12.

## CHRONOLOGY

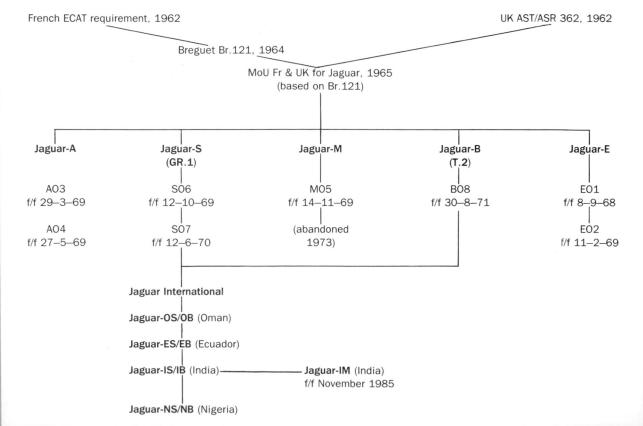

French ECAT requirement, 1962      UK AST/ASR 362, 1962

Breguet Br.121, 1964

MoU Fr & UK for Jaguar, 1965
(based on Br.121)

| Jaguar-A | Jaguar-S (GR.1) | Jaguar-M | Jaguar-B (T.2) | Jaguar-E |
|---|---|---|---|---|
| AO3 f/f 29–3–69 | SO6 f/f 12–10–69 | M05 f/f 14–11–69 | BO8 f/f 30–8–71 | EO1 f/f 8–9–68 |
| AO4 f/f 27–5–69 | SO7 f/f 12–6–70 | (abandoned 1973) | | EO2 f/f 11–2–69 |

Jaguar International

Jaguar-OS/OB (Oman)

Jaguar-ES/EB (Ecuador)

Jaguar-IS/IB (India) ——————— Jaguar-IM (India) f/f November 1985

Jaguar-NS/NB (Nigeria)

## PAINT AND CAMOUFLAGE

**L'Armée de l'Air:** Upper surfaces, gloss dark-grey and gloss dark-green; under surfaces, semi-gloss silver. Some aircraft deployed to Chad were finished in a desert scheme of sand and chocolate upper surfaces and sand or semi-gloss silver under surfaces. Interior faces of undercarriage doors and air brakes, matt greenish-yellow zinc chromate primer. Interior of air brake wells, exterior camouflage colours. General interior of cockpits, matt dark gull-grey (FS595a:26231) with a matt black floor. Instrument panel, matt black. Ejection seat, semi-gloss black with matt dark-grey headrest and matt dark-green harness. Undercarriage and leg struts, semi-gloss pale blue-grey (BS381C–697). Blade aerials, matt pale-yellow. Gunports, stained natural metal.

**Royal Air Force:** All-over 'wraparound' camouflage of dark sea-grey (BS381C-638) and dark-green (BS381C-641) in matt polyurethane. Original scheme had light aircraft grey (BS381C-627) undersides. Interior faces of undercarriage bays and doors, matt yellowish-green zinc chromate primer. Insides of air brakes and rest of air brake well, dark-green. Ejection seat, semi-gloss black with matt dark-green headrest. Lower rear fuselage aft of engine exhausts, matt blackish-brown stained metal. Tarnished metal gunports.

**Fuerza Aerea Ecuador:** As for original RAF scheme, only in matt acrylic.

**Indian Air Force:** As for original RAF scheme, only in matt acrylic. The Agave radar-equipped maritime strike aircraft are finished in dark sea-grey (BS381C-638) and light-grey (BS381C-631) upper surfaces and the same light-grey undersurfaces, in matt polyurethane.

**Nigerian Air Force:** A 'wraparound' scheme of mid-green (FS-595A-34159), dark-green (FS-595A-34079) and sand-brown (FS-595A-30318), in matt acrylic.

**Sultan of Oman's Air Force:** A 'wraparound' scheme of dark earth (BS381C-450) and light stone (BS381C-361), in matt acrylic.

## MODEL KITS AVAILABLE

| Manufacturer | Scale | Model | Markings |
| --- | --- | --- | --- |
| Airfix | 1:72 | Jaguar GR.1 | 54 Sqn RAF & SOAF |
| ESCI | 1:48 | Jaguar ? | ? |
| Frog (Novo) | 1:72 | Jaguar GR.1/T.2 | ? |
| Hasegawa | 1:72 | Jaguar-A-GR.1 | 54 Sqn RAF EC4/11 and Jaguar International demonstrator |
| Hasegawa | 1:72 | Jaguar-B/T.2 | 226 OCU, RAF, and EC2/7 |
| Heller | 1:100 | Jaguar-M | MO5 |
| Heller | 1:72 | Jaguar-A/B/E | EC1/7 + others |
| Matchbox | 1:72 | Jaguar GR.1 | 6 & 54 Sqns RAF |
| Matchbox | 1:72 | Jaguar T.2 | ETPS & SOAF |

**Alternative markings**
Modeldecal Range – all to 1:72 scale. Notes, photographs and drawings are included on the colour scheme and camouflage pattern, together with location of aircraft insignia. (The sheets identified here are not exclusively devoted to the Jaguars but contain a variety of other markings. In some cases, it is but a series of code latters, serial numbers and squadron insignia.)

*No. 29* Jaguar GR.1 (XX764) & T.2 (XX836), 14 Sqn RAF Bruggen, 1975.
*No. 30* Jaguar GR.1 (XX765) & T.2 (XX840), 17 Sqn RAF Bruggen, 1975.
*No. 32* Jaguar-As of EC1/7 (7-HF, A20), EC2/7 (7-PU, A10) & EC3/7 (7-IB, A47); Jaguar-Es of EC1/7 (7-HN, E13), EC2/7 (7-PJ, E21) & EC3/7 (7-ID, E18), St-Dizier, 1974–75.
*No. 38* Jaguar GR.1 (XZ104, 'N'; XZ107, 'R' or XZ109, 'O') of 2 Sqn RAF Laarbruch, 1976.
*No. 43* Two Jaguar GR.1s (XZ389 'CN') of 20 Sqn RAF Bruggen, 1977 and (XZ359 'M') of 41 Sqn RAF Coltishall, 1977.
*No. 46* Jaguar GR.1 (XX750, '22' or XX756, '07') 226 OCU RAF Lossiemouth, 1977.
*No. 50* Jaguar GR.1 (XZ387, 'DN') 31 Sqn RAF Bruggen, 1977.
*No 75* Jaguar GR.1 (XZ116, 'D') 41 Sqn RAF Coltishall, 1983.

**44.** This Jaguar-E of EC3/11 clearly shows the nose-mounted refuelling probe in place of the standard pitot tube. Note the worn paintwork on the leading edge of the wing and tailplanes. (AMD-BA)

44 ▼

**45.** The other airborne strike element of the Force d'Intervention Aérienne is provided by EC4/11 'Jura' based at Bordeaux-Mérignac. Here a Jaguar-A of the Escadron is seen at dispersal with an external fuel tank about to be winched below its belly. (SIRPA-Air)

**46.** EC4/11 is unique among Jaguar Escadrons of L'Armée de l'Air in that it is equipped with the Aérospatiale AS.30L laser-guided missile (seen here under each inner wing pylon). It uses the Thomson-CSF ATLIS II laser designator pod (under the aircraft centreline) to mark the missile's targets. (Aérospatiale)

▲45　▼46

**47.** One of the latest weapons to be qualified on the French Jaguar fleet is the 400kg laser-guided bomb (BGL 400), which uses a Matra *bombes à guidage laser* (BGL) kit fitted onto a standard 400kg bomb system. The kit consists of semi-folded tail fins and a front guidance kit. Between July 1988 and February 1989, seven test drops were carried out, all of which were successful. Two of these were in the United States during the Red Flag exercise. The BGL 400 can be delivered with accuracy up to 7km at low altitude and 13km at medium altitude. Here, two such weapons are seen on the inboard pylons of a Jaguar-B with a Matra Phimat chaff/flare dispenser on the outer port pylon and a Thomson-CSF Barem jamming pod on the outer starboard pylon. (CEV/Matra)

**48.** This photograph shows one of the first Jaguar GR.1s assigned to 226 Operational Conversion Unit (OCU) in 1973 based at RAF Lossiemouth. Although fitted with the fin fairing for the radar warning receiver (RWR), it has yet to be fitted with the 'chisel' nose housing the Ferranti laser ranger and marked target seeker (LRMTS). (MoD/OS.12)

**49.** This 226 OCU Jaguar GR.1 (without LRMTS) is seen in 1974 taxiing at Lossiemouth. The aircraft is equipped with underwing fuel tanks and two CBLS (Carrier, Bomb, Light Stores) units on the centreline pylon. (Tim Wrixon)

47▲　48▼

49▼

**50.** The second production Jaguar T.2 for the RAF landing at Lossiemouth. The robust undercarriage configuration, with twin main wheels on each leg is clearly visible, as are the nosewheel-door landing lights. (BAe Warton)

**51.** A line-up of RAF Jaguars of 226 OCU at RAF Lossiemouth in May 1974 shows that the LRMTS still has to be fitted to the GR.1s (identified by tail numbers). The T.2 trainers (identified by tail letters) have never been fitted with either LRMTS or RWR. (MoD/OS.12)

**52.** This 1975 photograph shows that the LRMTS still has to be fitted to 226 OCU aircraft, represented here by a GR.1 landing. The external fuel tank is mounted on the centreline pylon with the CBLS units on the outer wing pylons. (MoD/Rep-S)

**53.** One of 226 OCU's Jaguar GR.1As today. The RWR fairing on the fin carries a tartan marking along its length while the unit badge is visible on the air intake trunk. The Tracor ALE-40 chaff/flare dispenser can just be seen forward of the ventral fin under the rear fuselage. The aircraft has CBLS pods on the outer pylons. (Corporal D. Tomkins, RAF Lossiemouth)

**54.** The second RAF unit to form with the Jaguar was 6 Sqn in 1974 – initially at Lossiemouth, moving to its home at Coltishall later in the year. This view shows a single-seat GR.1A (after its mid-life update) fitted with a centreline fuel tank and, on each inner wing pylon, two 1,000lb bombs mounted on a tandem carrier, while the port outer pylon has the Westinghouse ALQ-101-10 ECM pod (known in the RAF as the Dash Ten pod) and on the starboard outer pylon (just visible) a Philips/Matra Phimat chaff dispenser pod. (Geoff Lee/BAe Kingston)

52▲    53▼

54▼

▲55 ▼56

**55.** No, the Jaguar force is not being pressed into the air defence role! This 6 Sqn aircraft is seen launching an AIM-9L Sidewinder air-to-air missile, carried for self-defence, from the port outer pylon. A Phimat chaff dispenser is carried on the starboard outer pylon, with 264-gallon drop tanks under the inner pylons. The two bulges just forward of the lower rear fuselage dorsal fins are Tracor chaff/flare dispensers. (BAe Kingston)

**56.** 'Twelve singletons and a T-bird!' The full strength of 6 Sqn is lined-up for the camera at Coltishall in July 1976. The squadron colours are visible along the RWR fairing at the top of the fin on the GR.1. This posed view is rare these days now that aircraft are assigned to individual, hardened aircraft shelters (HAS) dispersed around the airfield. (John Green/MoD)

▼57

**57.** Last of the UK-based RAF units to form in 1977, 41 Sqn has a dedicated reconnaissance role and is equipped with a recce pod under the centreline. Camera bays are located in the front and middle sections of the pod, allowing horizon-to-horizon coverage to be obtained as well as low and medium oblique coverage. The rear of the pod contains an infra-red linescan (IRLS) system. (41 Sqn)

**58.** A pair of 41 Sqn Jaguar GR.1 on the ground during an exercise in Norway. Compared with the previous and following photographs, one can hardly see the 'toned-down' squadron markings on the fin and air intakes. (Rolls-Royce, Leavesden)

**59.** This 41 Sqn Jaguar T.2 shows the wrap-around camouflage scheme and B-type insignia, but with the original red and white squadron insignia. The squadron is expected to re-equip with reconnaissance Tornados later in 1989. (41 Sqn)

58▲

59▲

**60.** The first RAF unit to equip with Jaguar was 54 Sqn, forming in March 1974 and moving to Coltishall in August of that year. This March 1984 photograph of a GR.1 shows the standard fit of external fuel tanks on the inner pylons and, on this occasion, CBLS on the outer pylons. (Author)

60▼

▲61

**61.** This recent view of a 54 Sqn GR.1 shows the tandem-mount for 1,000lb bombs on the inner pylons and the Westinghouse ALQ-101 ECM pod on the port outer pylon. The starboard outer pylon, not visible here, would carry an AIM-9 Sidewinder air-to-air missile (AAM) to enhance the Jaguar's self-defence capability in combat. (54 Sqn)

▼62

▼63

**62.** Every operational unit has at least one trainer version of the type on its strength; this Jaguar T.2 from 54 Sqn is seen taking-off during the Tactical Fighter Meet at Waddington in 1986. (RAF Waddington)

**63.** The other dedicated Jaguar reconnaissance unit is 2 Sqn (or II (AC) Sqn, as they prefer to see their 'numberplate' written — AC being the abbreviation for Army Cooperation). Based at Laarbruch, one of the RAF's 'clutch' bases in Germany, it was the last Jaguar unit in RAF Germany, re-equipping with the reconnaissance Tornado in January 1989. This view shows the wrap-around camouflage scheme clearly, as well as the standard fit of two external fuel tanks and the centreline recce pod. (Barry Ellson/RAFG-PR)

**64.** This photograph, showing a Jaguar T.2 of 2 Sqn, can be dated with absolute precision. With the author in the back seat (unrecognizable beneath his 'bonedome'), this aircraft followed a single-seat Jaguar on a low-level reconnaissance sortie over North Germany on 14 November 1978. This photograph was taken from the recce pod of the accompanying singleton. (2 Sqn)

**65.** The Jaguars in service with 2 Sqn were replaced by specially equipped Tornado GR.1s in early 1989. This formation shot was taken in 1982 to mark the 70th anniversary of the Squadron's formation on 13 May 1912. (Barry Ellson, RAFG-PR)

**66.** One of the four RAF Germany Jaguar units based at Bruggen during the late 1970s and early 1980s, 14 Sqn re-equipped with Tornados in 1985. This view shows a Jaguar GR.1 dropping four 1,000lb bombs from the centreline and outer pylons, with four more (in tandem mountings) on the inner pylons. (Geoff Lee/BAe Kingston)

64▲   65▼

66▼

**67.** Wearing only the squadron insignia on the air intakes, this 14 Sqn Jaguar T.2 poses for the BAC (now BAe) cameraman in 1975 as Bruggen's Station Commander, Group Captain J. R. Walker AFC, takes the aircraft over to Germany. (BAe Warton)

**68.** Following the Falklands experience in 1982, the RAF's Jaguar force was given a weapons update which saw an increased emphasis on self-defence. This 17 Sqn Jaguar GR.1 is seen mounting an AIM-9 Sidewinder AAM on the outer pylon. (Barry Ellson, RAFG-PR)

**69.** This view of a 17 Sqn Jaguar GR.1 shows the typical North German plain countryside over which they flew for ten years from 1975 until replaced by Tornados in 1985. The first letter of the two-letter code indicates the squadron and the second letter is the individual coding. (BAe Warton)

**70.** This pair of 20 Sqn Jaguar GR.1s shows the improved range of weapons and equipment given to the Jaguar in 1984. The top aircraft is carrying eight 1,000lb free-fall bombs; the lower aircraft has the external fuel tank mounted centrally with a pair of Paveway laser-guided bombs on the inner pylons. The outer port wing pylon is carrying an ALQ-101 ECM pod, and the starboard outer pylon has a Phimat chaff/flare dispenser. (Barry Ellson, RAFG-PR)

**71.** In 1977, 20 Sqn became the last RAF Germany unit to equip with the Jaguar, giving up its Harriers. This view shows the tanks on the inner pylons and a CBLS on the centreline. Squadron insignia is carried on the air intake and the aircraft coding on the fin. The squadron re-equipped with Tornado GR.1 in 1984. (Corporal Bob Clarke, RAFG-PR)

**72.** The fifth RAF Germany Jaguar unit was 31 Sqn, which re-equipped with the type in December 1975 and flew the Jaguar GR.1 until November 1984. It was based at RAF Bruggen. (Image in Industry)

**73.** A worm's eye-view of four Jaguar GR.1s from 31 Sqn on the flight line at RAF Bruggen. Note the various APUs and sundry ground equipment around the aircraft. Being based in Germany, all the emergency notices and signs on the aircraft are duplicated in German. (BAe Warton)

▲70  ▼71

**74.** Although the RAF does not formally operate a policy of flying Jaguars from dispersed sites, the type's ability to use motorways in time of war was demonstrated in the mid-1970s. Tim Ferguson, BAC Warton's Deputy Chief Test Pilot at the time, landed a Jaguar GR.1 in 450 yards on a stretch of the then new M55 motorway near Blackpool. After turn-round and re-arming with BL755 cluster bombs and underwing tanks, he took off again in 600 yards. (BAe Warton)

72▲ 73▼

74▼

▲75 ▼76 ▼77

▼78

**75.** In the late 1970s, using the UK trainer prototype BO8, XW586, BAC tested the use of a Thomson-CSF Agave radar, mounted in the front of a re-configured fuel tank. This radar allows the Jaguar to use anti-ship missiles such as the Aérospatiale AM.39 Exocet or BAe Dynamics Sea Eagle. (BAe Warton)

**76.** The Agave pod trials allowed BAe to offer the option of an attack radar for the Jaguar International model, seen displayed on the aircraft at the 1981 Paris air show. India has opted to configure one squadron's worth of Jaguars in this way, to offer a maritime strike capability, equipped with anti-ship missiles, believed to be Sea Eagle. (Author)

**77.** Another company-funded weapons development was the use of overwing pylons to carry the Matra R550 Magic 'dogfight' AAM. The installation is seen here mounted over the inner wing pylons. Although understood to be adopted by India, photographs of IAF

Jaguars in this configuration have yet to be seen. (BAe Warton)

**78.** Another view of the overwing Magic installation on Jaguar SO7 shows that use of this facility still allows a credible attack load (centreline fuel tank, inner BL755 cluster bombs and outer Matra SNEB rocket launchers) to be carried. (BAe Warton)

**79.** And just to prove the point . . . this sequence shows a Magic launch during the firing trials conducted in the late 1970s by British Aerospace. (BAe Warton)

**80.** Although the RAF equipped the Jaguar with early models of the AIM 9 Sidewinder, Oman requested clearance for using the AIM-9P version of Sidewinder. As with the RAF, the outer wing station was configured to carry the weapon, as illustrated. (BAe Warton)

79 ▲   80 ▼

▲81 ▼82

▼83

**81.** The first export sale for Jaguar was announced in August 1974 for two countries. Although they declined to be named or allow quantities to be revealed at that time, they were twelve each for Oman and Ecuador. The first aircraft, S(O)1, for the Sultan of Oman's Air Force (SOAF) – a single seater, equivalent to the RAF's GR.1 – is seen here taking-off from Warton on 7 March 1977. (BAe Warton)

**82.** The initial order for Jaguars from Oman was for ten single-seaters and a pair of B-model trainers. One of those two trainers (equivalent to the RAF's T.2) is seen here in wrap-around desert camouflage on its delivery flight in 1977. (BAe Warton)

**83.** The first unit of the SOAF to be equipped with Jaguar was 8 Sqn, based at Thumrait but now flying from Masirah Island. Lack of low-flying restrictions in vast areas of the Sultanate, allow the pilots to test their abilities to the full, as this photograph clearly illustrates. (BAe Warton)

**84.** A repeat batch of ten single-seaters and a pair of trainer Jaguars was ordered by Oman in 1980. Three of these aircraft, which equip 20 Sqn, SOAF, are seen here armed with the AIM,-9P for air defence duties. (BAe Warton)

**85.** Both SOAF Jaguar squadrons are now based at the former RAF base on Masirah Island. This photograph shows four 20 Sqn aircraft, again carrying the AIM-9P Sidewinder. (BAe Warton)

84 ▲

85 ▲

**86.** The second of the export launch customers announced in 1974 was Ecuador. The decision was a boost for the BAe sales team as it demonstrated Jaguar was able to operate in 'hot-and-high' environments. Here a single-seat Jaguar International of the Fuerza Aerea Ecuatoriana (FAE) is seen over the coast near Playas. (BAe Warton)

86 ▼

▲87 ▼88

▼89

**87.** Another view of an FAE Jaguar shows it flying over the high savannah of Ecuador. As far as can be ascertained the FAE has lost only one of the ten single-seaters and two trainers it acquired in the late 1970s. (BAe Warton)

**88.** This mid-1980s view of an FAE Jaguar International S model shows it taking off from Taura air base, some 40 kilometres east of Guayaquil. The aircraft is finished in the dark-grey/dark-green and light aircraft grey colours of the RAF. (BAe Warton)

**89.** India's choice of the Jaguar, beating the French Mirage F1 and the Swedish AJ37 Viggen, in October 1978, was the first export order to involve licence-production. Initially, however, twelve Jaguar GR.1s is from the RAF line were diverted to India to allow training to begin. Here an example of each interim Indian Jaguar is seen on a test flight before hand-over. All but three of the ex-RAF aircraft were subsequently returned to the UK. (BAe Warton)

**90.** A single-seat Jaguar and a trainer version prepare to take-off from their base in India in 1980. The Jaguar is now being built in total by HAL and recent reports from the sub-continent suggest a further 31 aircraft are to be ordered. (via BAe)

**91.** The Jaguar, known as the 'Shamsher' (Hindi for 'Brave Warrior'), entered Indian service with 14 Sqn IAF in 1980 and has since equipped three other units in the conventional strike role. This photograph shows a Maritime Jaguar (fitted with Agave radar and equipped to carry Sea Eagle missiles) flown by the fifth unit, 6 Sqn IAF, where they operate alongside Canberra B(I).12s as a composite unit. (via BAe)

**92.** This head-on view of a 6 Sqn IAF, Maritime Jaguar (not to be confused with the Jaguar-M) shows the smooth lines of the Agave radome in the nose of the aircraft. It is carrying 264 Imp gall external fuel tanks on the inboard wing pylons. It is assumed that a single Sea Eagle anti-ship missile is carried on the centreline pylon. (via BAe)

90▲ 91▼

92▼

▲ 93

**93.** The most recent export customer for the Jaguar was Nigeria. Originally, the potential order was seen as 36 aircraft, ▼ 94 but budgetary problems allowed only the first batch of eighteen aircraft to be contracted, in 1983. This photograph shows the first Jaguar International for the Nigerian Air Force on test in January 1984. Note the B-range serial registration G27-392 on the fuselage spine below the fin, which allows the aircraft to be flown in UK airspace. (BAe Warton)

▼ 95

**94.** This view of the same aircraft (NAF 705), one of the thirteen single-seaters ordered, shows to perfection the underside camouflage pattern of dark-green, mid-green and sand. Deliveries of the Nigerian order were completed in June 1985. (BAe Warton)

**95.** Five two-seat trainers were part of the Nigerian order. This evening photograph shows the first of them on the apron at Warton, prior to delivery. The robust nature of the undercarriage is evident. (BAe Warton)

96▲

**96.** As the RAF production order was coming to its end, a further two Jaguar T.2s were added to equip the Empire Test Pilot's School (EPTS) at Boscombe Down. Here the first of the two, XX915, is seen in the UK MoD (Procurement Executive) livery of red, white and blue, known universally as the 'Raspberry Ripple' scheme, at a Farnborough air show in the late-1970s. Following the loss of one of these two aircraft in 1981, a replacement aircraft was ordered, bringing total UK production to 203, plus prototypes. (Author)

**97.** In 1977 as part of the development towards what is now the European Fighter Aircraft (EFA), BAe converted a standard GR.1 to a fly-by-wire (FBW) control-configured vehicle (CCV). With a Marconi (now GEC) Avionics digital, quadriplex FBW system, this aircraft first flew on 20 October 1981. Having first flown in standard configuration, BAe added large wing leading-edge strakes in order to 'destabilize' the aircraft by ten per cent in the longitudinal axis. These strakes are evident in this view of the Jaguar FBW testbed coming in to land. (BAe Warton)

97▼

## The *Fotofax* series

A new range of pictorial studies of military subjects for the modeller, historian and enthusiast. Each title features a carefully-selected set of photographs plus a data section of facts and figures on the topic covered. With line drawings and detailed captioning, every volume represents a succinct and valuable study of the subject. New and forthcoming titles:

**Warbirds**
F-111 Aardvark
P-47 Thunderbolt
B-52 Stratofortress
Stuka!
Jaguar
US Strategic Air Power: Europe 1942–1945
Dornier Bombers
RAF in Germany

**Vintage Aircraft**
German Naval Air Service
Sopwith Camel
Fleet Air Arm, 1920–1939
German Bombers of WWI

**Soldiers**
World War One: 1914
World War One: 1915
World War One: 1916
Union Forces of the American Civil War
Confederate Forces of the American Civil War
Luftwaffe Uniforms
British Battledress 1945–1967 (2 vols)

**Warships**
Japanese Battleships, 1897–1945
Escort Carriers of World War Two
German Battleships, 1897–1945
Soviet Navy at War, 1941–1945
US Navy in World War Two, 1943–1944
US Navy, 1946–1980 (2 vols)
British Submarines of World War One

**Military Vehicles**
The Chieftain Tank
Soviet Mechanized Firepower Today
British Armoured Cars since 1945
NATO Armoured Fighting Vehicles
The Road to Berlin
NATO Support Vehicles

## The *Illustrated* series

The internationally successful range of photo albums devoted to current, recent and historic topics, compiled by leading authors and representing the best means of obtaining your own photo archive.

**Warbirds**
US Spyplanes
USAF Today
Strategic Bombers, 1945–1985
Air War over Germany
Mirage
US Naval and Marine Aircraft Today
USAAF in World War Two
B-17 Flying Fortress
Tornado
Junkers Bombers of World War Two
Argentine Air Forces in the Falklands Conflict
F-4 Phantom Vol II
Army Gunships in Vietnam
Soviet Air Power Today
F-105 Thunderchief
Fifty Classic Warbirds
Canberra and B-57
German Jets of World War Two

**Vintage Warbirds**
The Royal Flying Corps in World War One
German Army Air Service in World War One
RAF between the Wars
The Bristol Fighter
Fokker Fighters of World War One
Air War over Britain, 1914–1918
Nieuport Aircraft of World War One

**Tanks**
Israeli Tanks and Combat Vehicles
Operation Barbarossa
Afrika Korps
Self-Propelled Howitzers
British Army Combat Vehicles 1945 to the Present
The Churchill Tank
US Mechanized Firepower Today
Hitler's Panzers
Panzer Armee Afrika
US Marine Tanks in World War Two

**Warships**
The Royal Navy in 1980s
The US Navy Today
NATO Navies of the 1980s
British Destroyers in World War Two
Nuclear Powered Submarines
Soviet Navy Today
British Destroyers in World War One
The World's Aircraft Carriers, 1914–1945
The Russian Convoys, 1941–1945
The US Navy in World War Two
British Submarines in World War Two
British Cruisers in World War One
U-Boats of World War Two
Malta Convoys, 1940–1943

**Uniforms**
US Special Forces of World War Two
US Special Forces 1945 to the Present
The British Army in Northern Ireland
Israeli Defence Forces, 1948 to the Present
British Special Forces, 1945 to Present
US Army Uniforms Europe, 1944–1945
The French Foreign Legion
Modern American Soldier
Israeli Elite Units
US Airborne Forces of World War Two
The Boer War
The Commandos World War Two to the Present
Victorian Colonial Wars

A catalogue listing these series and other Arms & Armour Press titles is available on request from: Sales Department, Arms & Armour Press, Artillery House, Artillery Row, London SW1P 1RT.